Mental Health Raps

Bipolar and Manic Depressive Raps to Recovery inspired by Ice Cube, Eminem, Dr Dre, Snoop Dogg, 2 Pac, Sugar Hill Gang, Jay Z, NWA and every other rap artist out there who cares about madness

Jason Pegler

chipmunkapublishing
the mental health publisher

Jason Pegler

Published by
Chipmunkapublishing
PO Box 6872
Brentwood
Essex CM13 1ZT
United Kingdom

http://www.chipmunkapublishing.com

Chipmunkapublishing gratefully acknowledge the
support of Arts Council England.

Mental Health Raps, Writing for Recovery

Contents

Introduction

1st five rap albums lyrics:

1) A Can of Madness – whole album

2) Raps to Recovery – whole album

3) The Maddest Rapper In The World – whole album

4) Empowerment – One song only

5) Mad Ghetto – One song only

Jason Pegler

Mental Health Raps, Writing for Recovery

Introduction

Why a rap book?

I have always been inspired by music and rap has always been one of my favourite genre's. When I first heard NWA in 1988 I started to love rap. I liked the testerone pumped music and the wordplay and also the powerful messages you can convey in raps just as you can in stories.

The creativity and word play made me write one or two raps straight away and always made me interested in the music. I wrote a lot of poems/raps in 1992 when I was seventeen. A couple of thousand actually but through them all away when I was manic.

For me rap has always been a kind of empowerment and freedom of expression. I like a lot of rap anthems as well and see rap as a potential force for social good. It is something that can unite people, inspire people and even improve society if social messages come across in the music.

When I was younger I used to be really into Ice Cube and Snoop Doggy Dogg. I had posters of them on my wall at University. I played up to it a bit and lived a life full of booze, women and tended to get into a lot of fights. Over the years rap anthems have really inspired me to mellow out and give me hope.

For example Naughy By Nature's "Everything's gonna be All Right" used to really inspire me and chill me out. Also I liked some of the De La Soul stuff (more hip hop I know) and even PM Dawn's Set Adrift on Memory Bliss.

On my road to recovery Eminem played a big role. I would stand on my chair in my flat in Vauxhall and blast out Eminem learning all the lyrics to his contributions on Dr Dre's 2001 album and recited the main songs on 8 mile. I always felt Eminem was kind of his head and his lyrics really inspired me when I first started writing and helped me beat depression I think. Even though I was still manic a lot I have always felt that rap has given me a lot of energy and the mindset to want to have my own voice, give a voice to others and even to unite people who are excluded in some way.

I am no Gangster and never have been but I got into some scrapes and rap even now helps me release tension and helps my creativity.

I hope you enjoy the lyrics to my rap albums. My raps are available to buy on the Chipmunka website.

Happy hip hop and rap on.

100 Raps to Recovery

I'm writing a 100 raps to recovery
What the hell is this?
Yes .....
It's some kind of discovery
To raise awareness on mental health
And give us all some kind of real wealth
That is in your soul and not just your bank account
Because it's time to surmise,
Surprise and work out an account
Of how far you are prepared to go
To let all of the brothers know
What life is like inside the mind of a madman

Gonna stay pro-active and listen to the sad man
Was that s a a ad man or s A A D HA M M
Getting political now cause that's one way to go
If you wanna change the world then go with me
flow
Before other people die and the flowers they don't
grow

I'm looking into implementing regeneration
in Lambeth, that's for Equal Lives
Gonna sort out my own borough, then do one at a
time
Want to help Southwark out but they are doing real
well
And my head starts spinning and my mind's in hell
Cause if I see too much suffering I'll be back in the
bin
Like being dropped by vintage Mike Tyson and landed
on the chin

The rap above shows how difficult it is to help others when you are struggling yourself. What's needed is pro-activity, strategic planning, a good heart and good people amongst other things. For some it is too late, but they too still inspire and can leave their legacies.

Mental Health Raps, Writing for Recovery

Second Rap to Recovery

Starting my second 100 rap to recovery on
Christmas Eve
I've got many pieces of armoury hidden in me
sleeve
Too late for Pete Shaugnessey I do believe
(Respect – Respect to this man – he did what very
few others can)
An inspirational super user who helped people
breathe
Gonna gain more momentum now that he has gone
May the force be with me like Luke Skywalker and
OB1
Madpride and A Can of Madness they are one
of a kind
Neither of them is afraid to speak their own mind
Gonna save the user movement at the end of the
day
All of these individuals are cherished by us
survivors   in some way
Now I've made my point I hope I can hear you
asking
How can I really help instead of multi tasking?
First you must make sure you can look after
yourself
It's unfair to bring your burdens onto someone
else's shelf
When your mind is steady and you're ready for
action
Send me an email and we'll start the contractions
Breathe in for Chipmunkapublishing and out for
Equality

These are both my creative visions, a social
enterprise and a utopian ideal
Chipmunka publishes the stories of the mentally
insane
Equality helps the poor communities who've
suffered similar pain
Both give the opportunity to live a better life than
before
So there's still hope for you if you listened to too
much hardcore
So if you see a rap event in your local
neighbourhood
Look out for the Renegade Artistry and Raskil
Records who are doing some good
Like Chipmunkapublishing we are saving lives

Meanwhile Jamie, a fellow manic I'd met in a coffee
shop in Green Park in February 2003, had done my
first portrait. It inspired me to publish my third rap to
recovery which I started to write in his presence.

I'm looking at the picture and it's got to be said
This guy is a manic he looks off his head
Yet controlled in some way me thinks as well
Keep rapping and drawing like this we'll be
doing swell
Against the odds and we're one of a kind
The start of equality for the mentally ill I hope you
find
Like gay people started to be accepted when I was
growing up
I turned to drink as an unaccepted manic but kept
from throwing up

Mental Health Raps, Writing for Recovery

Felt so much pain that I made my stomach so
strong
On the outskirts was tough on the inside was
wrong
Took years to accept it then I got right
Determined to spend the rest of my life making a
fight
For the rights of the mentally insane
Whatever happens it will not be in vain
There's a connection with us manics like a
parallel universe
The status quo is scared so it places a curse
But anything that's misunderstood is treated this
way
Rise up to the challenge and win the day
Educate the media and public and fight for
Equal Lives
We'll go Gandhi way before we use knives
How will we they treat us in 50 years time
Will they be embarrassed to be a friend of mine?
We're all human at the end of the day
A slight change in psychology then we've made our
point
People will have empathy no need to smoke a joint
Eliminating psychiatry with the help of psychiatry
itself
An ideal to strive for to contribute to our mental
wealth
Our mental health is getting better every single day
I hope to share this with millions of people
When we have the mental health live aid one day
This will be my first global rap performance in
public live

Jason Pegler

I'm a buzzing messenger from the mental health
hive
You try to get rid of us we'll sting you back
We fight for equality from the average hacks
Too many people and faces are fighting together
A community growing forever and ever

Raps to Recovery Album

Lyrics from the First rap Album A Can of Madness

Any lyrics written below are not meant to upset anyone or incite any kind of violence. The lyrics were written whilst I was on psychiatric drugs and were the beginning of the development of my style as a rap artist. Any reference to language that could be deemed offensive has been published to illustrate my feelings whilst experiencing side effects on various medications. I believe that rap music can be used as a means for freedom of expression and is therefore a force for social good.

**The Jason Pegler Announcement –
Raps to recovery**

Anyone trying to use the work of MC Jase will be crucified. Need I say you?! That includes you, Mr Mel Gibson, your father and Quentin Tarantino – unless you pay Jason Pegler 21/02/75 that's 21/02/75, 1 billion dollars up front and reduce world suicide you're at it.

MC JASE

I'm MC Jase
And I'm off my face
With my Mace
I'm a headcase
Certified as a nutter when I was 17 years old
Right now I've got hair no cancer so I'm not bold.
Enough to feel sorry for myself
This MC is always full of stealth
Leading an army empowering mental health
Taking time to build up my strength
Using different media types and length
Whole empire is growing by word of mouth
First North, West, East and finally South.
Too many tasks for the multi skilled
Keep observing others then get off those pills
3 months more of Quetiapine
3 years of Valporate then off the gin
Back to reality, human being again
Diary of a madman discriminatory like man.
Creative voice is heard in prose
Better than breaking somebody's nose.

3/4/01 Poll Vault

Here's a tune for vault recordings, you know who I
mean.
I've been to fuckin' prison, at least, I might as well
have been.
We're a hot new record label with lots of wicked
stuff,
so if you've been listening to shit, we think you've
had enough.
I've been rapping for a while, in lots of different
ways.
Been through more shit than Eminem & I'm not
afraid of gays.
I've seen a world of madness, where most people
couldn't go,
and occasionally I return, when my mind goes to
and fro.

I've got madness on the brain
(Cypress Hill thought they were insane)
and I know it causes pain,
But, I have to tell my homies,
'cause my thoughts drive me insane.

I saw violence growing up, in my home and
neighbourhood.
I used to get badly picked on cause, my brain was
fuckin' good.
There were NWA and 2 Live Crew for a teenager
growing up
The only sense of security was my Alsatian pup.
There was petty crime and drug dealing that I
undertook.

Mental Health Raps, Writing for Recovery

Sometimes I was rather fortunate to get off the
hook.
There were women everywhere but not as many as
Snoop,
and I've been so fucking sick; I'm still waiting for my
coup.

I've got madness on the brain
and I know it causes pain.
But, I have to tell my homies,
to stop them from doing the same

I remember knocking out a copper, when my mate
lived in a squat,
I was so fucking paranoid; I thought the place was
hot.
When I told my teacher that I was dealing drugs at
school,
she burst out crying and said that she felt like a
fool.
I had a good education and didn't take advantage
of it,
now I realise I was fortunate, and that I'd acted like
a tit.
Never used to go to school, I would lie there in my
bed.
If I had my time again, I know the books I would
have read.

I've got madness on the brain (and it's driving me
insane),
getting better at the game,
And I have to tell my homies,
to stop them from having the same.

Jason Pegler

Had so many fights, it's impossible to add them up,
won them all apart from one, but I never had a cup.
A sovereign ring broke my nose and I broke my jaw myself,
the scar on my face from a screwdriver arose from clumsy stealth.
So I've been through loads of agro and now I've quietened down,
and if you try to wind me up, I'll probably just frown.
Don't push me or my crew too far, cause you will never know,
how far we've come and been, and how far we're willing to go.

Seen madness now I'm tame (it was driving me insane),
getting better at the game.
And I have to tell my homies,
cause they've helped make MC Jase's fame.

When I operate on the mike, there are many things to do,
philosophise and educate, but mostly, I entertain all of you.
There were bad things in my early days,
but now I've changed my ways.
Now I'm a real citizen,
as the past becomes a haze.
Still mentally insane, and it's a shame, I'm not to blame.
'Cause it causes so much pain, to tell people my real name.

Mental Health Raps, Writing for Recovery

Must stay on medication, so I can rejoin my
generation,
must not forget, or relapse, or I could embarrass
the X.

I've seen madness; now I abstain (slow)
I've already made my claim.
I thank my homies, then and now,
for putting up with my burning flame.

Gotta get it right for the world,
make it all a better place.
And then it will be worthwhile, to have rapped.......
yours truly.......the lyricist........and MC Jase.

Jason Pegler

19/06/01 Alcohol

Things were going wrong when I used to hit the
bottle
Used to sit there and talk about who I'd throttle
Now there's homies round these flats
And everywhere I go I'm surrounded by twats
But at least they know their hip hop
And I know I'm going to the top
Of the rap music industry
That's DJ Fraudster and me
The vauxhall boys gonna take over
A rapper and a composer
We don't give a fuck about no life
That's only covered in strife
Might as well just end it all now
Than try to figure out how
But then I guess that'd be copping out
And we're made of metal there's no doubt
We're gonna crucify the rest
Because together we're the best
Whether it's free style or rehearsed
Our magic bubble gonna burst
And we're grateful to Eminem
That mad rapper can be a gem
He's bringing hip hop over here
And that makes it really clear
That we're gonna go for it
Because we've been through too much shit
We're gonna bounce back off the mike
And mix some tunes that give a spike
Cause we're really into this game
And we really want and need that fame, MC Jase

Mental Health Raps, Writing for Recovery

Rhyme and Reason

Rhythm, rhyme and <u>reason,</u> is for all of the four
<u>seasons</u>
So when this rapper wants to <u>show</u> which route
he's gonna <u>go</u>
There's some logic in his <u>mind</u> and a story you will
find
About the <u>world</u>.
Yeah the <u>world</u> and what it's like
About life; and all the <u>strife</u>.
About how to cope with it, instead of feeling shit
The troubles that begin
Whether big, fair, huge or thin
This rappers really gonna be
No 1 for eternity + philosophy
Cause I got poetry that makes <u>sense</u>
An understanding of anthropology that's <u>intense</u>
I gotta hold of the mike and I won't let go
Wanna make me famous and make some dough
So I can set myself up and my future family
(speed up) And prepare for any traumas that may
affect me
Gonna entertain the crowd in a different way
No bullshit, or gangster rap but memories from the
day
Tunes that will stay in peoples minds
And words that are targeted to open blinds

Cause I want people to learn from doing wrong
And I want them to sing this song
I want their lives to be fulfilled
I don't preach, I'm just chilled

(Slow) out. That's child out.
And I've been there,
well into despair.
And I got out. Just about
and it was hard, to play my last card.
I kept guard and although my life was marred,
I escaped to have my music taped
And then a record deal,
hoes, nice suits and a flash car.

Mental Health Raps, Writing for Recovery

Vauxhall Crew

Rapping now for the Vauxhall generation
Dolly Sen's drum and bass, the new sensation
Council estates must get rid of crack
And get these broken community spirits back.
Time for the hardcore music to make sense at last
Things boring, normal, then too fast.
I'm just a manic depressive at the end of the day
Want me to get a job and join society, no way.
Too much stigma and discrimination going on
round here
Feel guilty for mentioning it, must drink beer.
Something's not quite right me, rapping here today.
I'm white, manic, not homophobic or gay; at least
that's what I say.
Social evolution is what's happening now
Multicultural society ends the racism row
Equal lives must unite across the universe
Positively helping the status quos perversed
I'm so tired now I could end my life
Preaching like a bell end about my strife
Mental illness is a horrible thing
Mentally ill in Amityville makes my ticker ringer
Laughing at reality is an ingenious way
To forget the fucking label that ruins my day
My friend jumped off a bridge not so long ago
Couldn't stop that but with these words I grow
Next time you see a schizophrenic in the paper
OPEN YOUR FUCKING MIND!
DON'T LEAVE THESE LUNATICS BEHIND!
Help them out
Cause we're all human beings at
The end of the day

Jason Pegler

Even us Manic Depressives
Who don't know what to SAY?

Time to heal

There's still time to heal. Time to heal, for real. Stop making bad motherfucka's and be more like brothers. So there's time to heal for real, and bad motherfucka's can turn into brothers. That's turn motherfucka's into brothers.

There's racism all over the world, so rap is everywhere.
Just listen to a great rapper, and tell me that you don't care.
They'll fill your mind full of truth, intensity, love and questions
That's with philosophy, psychology and their best intentions.

And in multicultural societies all over the globe,
rap is a language that can reach everyone's abode.
Get rid of the gangster rap lifestyle, that people aspire to,
and substitute it for real rapping, that makes people do what they do.

We can still keep the element of fun, shock and crazy shit,
but rid the world from images of nigga's causing all the shit.

Blacks have been oppressed and that's a fact,
time they made amends instead of getting whacked.
And if it takes a mad white man, to help them along their way,

Then so be it, I dedicate myself.
I don't care if people think I'm gay.
And I don't care if people think that I'm wasting my time
It's all mine and I'll do it without expecting a dime.
Because it's my craving out of a necessity,
want to help solve the disease I see,
People not together and fighting each other's ass,
when all they need to do is hut, hut, hut, look up and pass.

Yeah. Pass the ball to each other
And turn the bad mother fucker's into brothers.
Cause there's still time to heal.
Time to heal for real.
And I want to stop bad mother fuckers
and help turn them into brothers.
Then us brothers, can say thank you, to our mothers.

So next time you're burning some weed and listening to death row,
remember that if a brother pulls out a g-lock its time to go.
No need to hang around and act too tough,
Because one thing is for sure,
you've both already suffered enough.
Once you get away from the violence and killing,
can start enjoying things, and make life more fulfilling.
There are so many things, out there to do.
It's a tragedy to die young, a tragedy for you.
70% of rap records are bought by middle class whites,

so there's hope for the rest of us and room for more
party invites.

Yeah. Pass the ball to each other
And turn the bad mother fucker's into brothers.
Cause there's still time to heal,
time to heal for real.
And I want to stop bad mother fuckers,
and help turn them into brothers.
Then us brothers, can say thank you, to our
mothers.

As this rapper starts out his career,
there's one thing you should know.
He's gonna rhyme like kid n play and know exactly
when to let go
Of the mic to let the melody and backing vocals
intervene

Cause he has an intuitive understanding of
narrating the obscene
That's a comical element of rap that is always here
to stay
As there's nothing wrong with healthy sex not even
if you're gay
Better to have a world full of orgies and open
sexuality
Than one based on vengeance
and shooting mother fuckers in the knee.

Juice and Gin

When you Dogg Pound Crew gonna let JCB come
in?
I've spent all this time sipping on juice and Gin.
And I see the great Eminem,
so cool that he can't rap about race
Well I'm not afraid, 'cause I've been to every place.
Know what it's like to be mad, then you know what I
mean.
I've endured it and recovered from it, you should
have seen

SEEN IT.
Seen the shit.
And I've endured it.
And I've still got my wit

My heads going to explode 'cause I write raps so
quick.
And I've got no boundaries, so I'm gonna make you
sick.
And tell you of all the troubles in the world, that
2pac talks about.
And I'll be accurate as well, of that...there is no
doubt.

About drugs, a life of crime (pause) bitches,
money and a life of irresponsibility (27)
About guns, sex, fighting, booze, prison,
and love, decisions and insecurity. (20)
There's nothing I won't tell.
I'll tell everything that's on my mind.
My honesty bodes well,

Mental Health Raps, Writing for Recovery

at least, that's what I hope you'll find.

Cause life's hit me so hard I've no longer got a
guard.
I'm opening my heart for the benefit of art.
A music known as rap,
which upper class people think is crap.
But its music that is real,
that's music that you can feel.
Not like that ancient shit,
that makes me have a fit

Rap makes one feel at home...unlike the
millennium dome.
It's more valuable than chrome.
Yes, more valuable than Rome

Rap is a kind of music that is here to stay.
Its essence is too important, for it to ever go away.
Compounding more out of racism in 60's America.
There are many scars that I'll be telling ya.
These mother fucka's ain't healed yet.
If you think they have, you're a fool, I'll bet.
Black people had a rough time at the hands of
whites,
and their bound to want revenge from societies ugly
shites.
Remember when a black man couldn't go in the
same bar as a white,
well it takes a long time and a lot of education to
forget that shite.

In time, generations can forgive that shit,
and rap is the only mass way to convey it bit by bit,

Jason Pegler

For church ain't that popular anymore,
it's too antiquated for the young.
They're more likely to get pissed off, get hold of a
gun.
Get the bastards back for making them hooked on
crack,
for if you move to the hood it's hard to get back on
track.
There's a lot of discipline needed to make a good
rapper,
need to educate, without preaching, and entertain
the foot tapper.

Mental Health Raps, Writing for Recovery

JCB 1

Now ev-ery body <u>listen</u>… to me
Stepping up on this mike… is <u>JCB</u>
Joining my crew… is the thing to do
(That means) telling other people what happened to
you
Honesty is the name of the game
Making other's feel the (empathy) for your pain.

It's time to take the ride that was slip – er, ey.
As Coolio did it, then so can we
No need for the gin we just need the juice
Cause Snoop Doggy Dogg is a bit different than
Proust
He may (be the best) rapper that's still alive
But sometimes (that gangsta stuff stings) <u>like</u> a
beehive

It can, encourage youngsters to get the wrong end
of the stick
Make them sell crack and think through their dicks
Causing teenage pregnancy on the estates
Making life even harder than social policy dictates
Black people born into poverty all the time
Not surprising is it – really – that there's so much
crime

I ran 100 miles to see NWA
Then the Fugees made me stop and find another
way,
Developed my own philosophy to help the
disadvantaged,
Reflected on my life – knew I was privileged,

Jason Pegler

2pac gave me strength to make my quest reality
Although he is dead he gives me psychic energy

Like O B 1 <u>Kenobie</u> in the (star wars trilogy)
let Darth-Vader <u>win</u> to deceive his enemy.
<u>Luke</u> felt the force and got stronger every day,
JCB will win YES I'm going to save the day!

Going to stomp all the crime by reducing ignorance,
First, bring different cultures together – give them
all significance.
Lots of ways to do this – make them part of the UK,
join up with So Solid Crew – they may behave in a
different way.
They describe things as they've seen them in
Battersea they say,
so I give them my respect – now I should tell you
about myself.

Born and bred in Gloucester with sex, drugs,
booze, and women
Everything seemed stable until I developed manic
depression.
Trying to stop a nuclear war that was only in my
mind,
making all these assumptions that I could never
find.
Went from mania to paranoia at the click of a manic
gun,
I was certified a madman, therefore crazier than
everyone.

Mental Health Raps, Writing for Recovery

When JCB was seventeen I was hospitalised for
my mental health.
In the years to follow this would seriously affect my
wealth.
Really hit rock bottom when I realised what I'd
thought,
one minute saving the world then humiliated and
distraught.
Spent six months mad and suicidal in a mental
institution,
a miscarriage of justice planted the seeds for a
revolution

Diagnosed with a mental illness it took ten years to
accept it

I managed to sort my head out for the very first
time...

Start bringing different cultures together and
making them chime.

A Can of Madness

Now, I was forced to go into a mental asylum,
at seventeen years of age,
And some years later I wrote about it
and cried on every page.
It was not recalling the experience itself that made
me really weak,
but telling people about it and letting them here me
speak.

I spent a long time writing and getting my book
published.
The government gave me funding which stopped
me feeling dissed.
I would give the first 300 sales to charity,
Fuck me, thanks to mind,
I'd been given an opportunity.

There are so many things in life that I want to
achieve.
But I only get so much time so it's difficult to
alleviate the pressure,
as I don't know where to prioritise
Cause I don't know about all that gangster shit,
I don't feel wise.

I grew up in Gloucester,
which I thought was really good
Cause there were so many nutters in my
neighbourhood.
Then one day I grew up and realised,
it was all an urban joke

Mental Health Raps, Writing for Recovery

Cause by the time I left, I'd kicked the fuck,
out of almost every bloke

Then I went to Manchester, to go to University
I was meant to study Classics but I tried to be a G.
With my mates working on the door, and me
shifting my shit,
Life was made more fruitful with a regular piece of
clit.

There were bitches and hoes more regular than
before,
And it was nice to be called a stud,
instead of a fucking whore.
I was popular at Uni,
till my drinking took control.
I'd have six litres of strong cider,
then piss on the remote control

I was violent all the time, and generally depressed.
But when I played football I had the talent of
George Best.
There were many things going on when we lived in
Mosside.
Living next door to a borstal helped make us the
law abide.

You see this started moral questions going on in
my mind.
I became too drunk to do anything evil for mankind.
Recovery wouldn't happen for several years,
that's why my fucking memoir is so full of tears.

Jase August 8th 2001

Jason Pegler

Where is love

I was white now I'm black
In this multicultural trap
There's a vision of the world I have as well
To combat prejudice and stigma and remove this
hell
A manic man, who's too scared to say it,
Once he reveals he'll have to pay for it

But the world is changing and societies gotta
answer
Got me homies with me and my ghetto blaster
Doin' the right thing for the segregated
You are of the alienation that you've created
Accept people for what they are when you meet
them
Don't judge pre-emp or abuse or try to defeat them

Where's the black representation in this society
Gangsta rappa's and priests only is not diversity
Everyone else come out of your shell
Let bygones by bygones we might as well.

Ode to Slim Shady

Eminem can fuck it
I'll saw his head off
and put it in a bucket

People call him the rabbit
That makes me Big Wig
god damn it
I can run 8 million miles
So watch it!
Hang on let me think
I can't saw my idol's head off
That would be very disconcerting.

Ode to Slim Shady 2

Been rappin 10 minutes,
Eminem can shit it.
Been a manic depressive since 17
and he thinks he's losing it.
Ain't got not grit for a bit, or a tit
I'm beat, I was neat,
but popped pills and was defeated.
Sorry Shady. Loving you really. My head is in
pieces.

Ode to Slim Shady 3

Eminem I want to love you
But my hearts not full of shit
There's people dying shady
And you joke in spite of it
My dad can't understand you

His wife thinks you're a Dog
I'm understanding what you mean
But you got to do it my way now shady.
My ego is dying now. Thank God. You are the best
Slim. And thanks for saving my life.

Ode to Slim Shady 2009

I used to rap to Eminem in my living room
Rehearsing his songs with a manic mind at the top
of my voice
Hundreds of neighbours could hear but no-one
complained
A manic man learning to survive by imitating one of
his idols. Not imitated like that since NWA and
Straight Outta Compton.
I'm here for you slim should you ever need support
You contributed to saving my live and thanks to
you, please allow me to retort
You gave me the strength to others support.

---

8 Billion Miles

Another rap to recovery is stepping up tonight,
Regenerating the urban generation used to give me
a fright,
Now it's an automatic humanitarian goal,
To take the community in and its heart and soul,
MC Jase alive returning to the house that Jack
thought he built,
Too many mistakes in the box and they're covered
in guilt,
Manufactured rappers not writing their own lyrics,
Feeling sorry for themselves their bullies and
cynics,
Waiting for the sunlight to rise on this beautiful day,
Gonna stop this gangster rap nonsense and spread
positivity my way,
Twenty four hours till things turn around,
Humanitarian goals for your breath, sight and
sound,
Not born in the ghetto but been to hell and back,
Caused by ecstasy and a manic depressive attack,
Eight years after then I bounced back,
Cured myself and helped others to heal,
Thought I was crazy when I listened to Seal,
He's had his head together all this time,
With those mushrooms and strawberries,
Pink New Yorkers and awful hash coffees.
One street brawl lost and the next 50 won,
My life nearly ended before it begun,
Things going on, people too scared to face up to
want their dream,
Receiving your destinies, easy, just don't let your
brain steam,

Jason Pegler

Life is worth living don't ask me that question,
Stop using other models; make your own invention,
Equal lives for all and Chipmunks unite,
Publishing, media, film, internet and your fight,
To make things open up, door and front,
Smile, laugh, do a parachute jump.

Mental Health Raps, Writing for Recovery

Lyrics from my second Rap Album Raps To Recovery.

I have decided in this stage of the book to illustrate how creative writing has been an empowering process for me throughout the last few years. Writing is still an empowering process for me. Writing helps my sanity, helps me develop my thoughts and views and enables me to get my messages and inner most thoughts across.

The lyrics of these rap's were written between 2005 and 2009, so some of the views may be dated or as is sometimes the case with writing momentary. Raps give me an outlet for creative expression. I used to write a lot of poetry but have preferred writing raps over the last few years. I've liked listening to rap ever since I was about thirteen and listening to NWA. Writing rap is similar to other forms of writing, as when we write it represents how we feel at a moment in time. On some issues our perception and views may develop or change. Other times they will not.

None of these raps are meant to offend, so I apologise beforehand if any of them do. Some of them are quite intense. Writing the raps was cathartic and publishing them is empowering for me, so here it goes.

Please also allow a little creative license. Rapping etiquette involves battling and challenging and even insulting others although on the whole the raps are

Jason Pegler

pretty positive I think and I tried to tone them down
a bit for this book.

Chipmunka Hop

Welcome to the chipmunka hop, partying so hard
never going to stop,
Living life to enjoy it until the end, if your spirit's
broken, together we will mend.
You been a drop out for too long, then sing along to
the chipmunka song,
Do the chipmunka shop and battle for yourself and
empower everyone.
Visualise a world where everyone is healthy and
happy, united forever
chipmunka hopping and shopping together, we
Gonna stop... never,
Hopping til the end of time and shopping with twine
in the sublime.
Ladies come on and dance to this, together we can
create bliss,
Making the world a better place and getting off our
face,
With a natural love for life waking up the house is
mc jase.

Welcome to the chipmunka hop, partying so hard
never going to stop,
Living life to enjoy it until the end, if your spirits
broken together we will mend,
You can live your life again, make it better than
before and stay forever on the dance floor.

Jason Pegler Rap

You want to rap about reality then that's fine with
me,
Make a story up and you'll get found out, I won't let
it be.
I'm jason pegler the master of self discovery, you
wont forget, you'll see.
If you're adding positivity to the game, you are
entitled to your fame,
If you're taking more than you're giving and people
are suffering,
Jason Pegler is the name to dread, making you red,
putting bad rappers to bed.
Enough said, before I shred your head, place you in
a psychiatric bed,
Pump you full of drugs and alter your mindsets,
leaving your brain dead.
I spent 12 years as a manic depressive in a living
hell,
So you think I give a f*** about people dissing me?
Time will tell,
I'll be ringing the victory bell, and unloading my
shell, selling platinum records in the new game until
the end of time, busting my rhymes,
Stopping others crimes and giving others a life line

I'm Jason Pegler, creating new weather at the end
of my tether,
Creating rap harmony as a force for social good
forever and ever.
A white nutter, with a black heart brothers,

Mental Health Raps, Writing for Recovery

Rappers Delighted

Rapping from the ghetto, delighted with these echoes,
A social underclass is rising from the manic streets of London,
A Vauxhall resident flawed, who cured myself,
On my way to emotional freedom and eternal health.
Rappers delighted, let's hope were united,
I'm on your side, unless you blow my hide,
Then I will reside on your bad assed face and metamorphose.
From Jason Pegler into JCB and manic jase,
A metaphoric threat as recovering others first made me fear death,
Now my resolve is secure, 20,000 hardcore really did knock at my door.
6 billion of us alive, rapping to the fore,
Classical inspiration, choose if you want more.
30 years of age and opening the page,
To a world of personal transformation,
Encouraging the United Nations,
To enable the third world to stand up and seize salvation.
Injustice, from global warming to degrading the poor,
Whatever spin is used we know the truth, give more.
Stop illegally crippling Africa and Asia alike,
Before 10 million rappers bust your criminality and ignite this revolutionary fight.
Rappers of the world delighted, the United Nations united, inspired by artists online, raising awareness

of the oppressed, Jason Pegler's curing madness is next,
And then context, in effect, the hip hop generation x, empowering the oppressed, with technology in effect,
For the select crew of honesty, using rhymes like woven floristry and seniority, to eradicate unheard of minorities and make democracy the majority where the poor get powerful and the rich give back,
Turn off the mic, rappers delighted...
Rat a tat tat, 2 Pac words have had a massive impact and the Sugar Hill Gang Symphony has my respect as its own initiative, I'm just being myself not a derivative,
Jason Pegler bows out as an initiative like a sieve, so please embrace and give.

Mental Health Raps, Writing for Recovery

Who Are You?

A prolific rapper in the third person empowering you
So much already done and gone and even more to do.
Fixing society as a rapper 24-7, here's showing you how.
Removing my own ego and being right here right now.
These lyrical dancing rhymes are one of a kind,
Reality making you blind? Make up your own mind.
Social rhetoric back to front, this yoke has egg in it,
Introverted, ego maniacal mania for the self converted.
Life is about living and it's always worth doing it,
Thinking for yourself before you've become part of the matrix.
Rapping to reduce discrimination on humanitarian grounds,
Winning away from home the odds in favour to hit those rebounds,
Physiology's important and leaving one's soul fulfilled,
Knowing yourself. I'm thrilled, and self grilled.
To 6 billion degrees centigrade,
And I still feel like vanilla ice... played.
Reversing the mic to make social anthropology emerge from the haze.
Been rapping for well being non stop for 30 years in various ways.
Society is full of hope and promise so release yourself and discover,
Who you are? Just be it don't ask a question

Fulfil your life with your self not voyeuristic
intentions,
Common sense climaxes your own erection
Who are you really? Reverse the rhetorical
question,
Upon reflection,
dismiss the inflection and add honesty and
incantation to your record collection, patent yourself
before someone's walked off with your selection or
hand over and diversify your cry to live the life you
want to and don't decry, or deny, no need to apply
just do it and don't leave yourself dry before you die
and rejoin with a new high...

Cured Myself

I've cured myself what you gonna do about that?
rat a tat tat !
I arose from clumsy stealth and not on the drugs
any more you brats.
You've been lying to billions of people around the
globe.
Now I have to name you all, but first let me put on
my boxing robe.
Drug companies surrounding the world on a
mission to succeed,
To help their patients we think like children in need.
There wouldn't be a vested interest in there for you,
I hear you shudder,
This rappers aware of it and has planted the seeds
for your downfall you mother f******. I hear you say.
I think I'll make a drug that will make people
addicted,
For better or worse I really don't give a f***, I'm in
luck, will make me a quick buck.
I picture you rolling this in your off shore bank
accounts no more
I have been sending players out, documenting your
criminal hardcore,
I know the score, and leading this uproar, for sure,
forever more.

With the drugs you force fed me I nearly gave in,
Most people are hooked or either in the bin,
You didn't bank on me sipping on juice and gin.
Jason Pegler is alive and will kick your heads in,
So the world can know the truth and people can be
themselves again.

Then I'll snap back to reality, not losing my gravity,
And not being addicted to sleeping tablets,
Like the great Eminem who is someone else you
f***** up,
Just like the history of the people of the world and
their mental health,
F*** me, that's just about every g, how long until
your in captivity ?
With a reversal in fortune what goes around comes
around,
So if your innocent, or did it unwittingly a pound for
a pound,
Otherwise your history, and I'll make you a
character in a gangster movie for sight and sound,
Cured myself and survived the suicidal side effects.
Cash for 12 years lost of a life please... whose
next?
Get in touch with me and together we'll all be free,
you're hexed.
Can't silence me, I've been cloned in every multi
media format,
And we're all over the internet and in the streets,
now you know that:
Drug companies bow to your knees, psychiatry f***
off please.
If there has been malpractice in your mental health
services or system shudder at your f****** knees, I
am the thunder, no need to wonder,
To late for your blunders! Stop. C to the H to the I
to the P to the M to the U to the N to the K to the A
spells Chipmunka. Stop. Look. Listen. Relax. Write
about it and forgive...

Mental Health Raps, Writing for Recovery

Curing myself, for health not money, world justice
and our mental health

With the drugs you force fed me I nearly gave in,
Most people are hooked or either in the bin,
You didn't bank on me sipping on juice and gin.
Jason Pegler is alive and will kick your heads in,
So the world can know the truth and people can be
themselves again.

Giving love in the house tonight, spare a thought for
others and unite,
Join our fight to stand up for the rights of the
abused and confused.

Together we can lift them and bring peace to the
human race,
Jason Pegler rapping for peace and love, every
body in the place.
Turn up the bass and metamorphose into a unified
headspace,
Driving a spiritual light upon the dawn of the j peg
era,
Stopping the burning of pain like aloe Vera, coming
near ya.

We're giving love tonight to spare a thought for
others and unite,
Join our fight to stand up for the rights of the
abused and confused,

As a team we can use the world music scene as a
go between,

Jason Pegler

To democratise the human race by allowing the
third world to show its face.
African rights to be grasped for eternity, stand down
Mgabee,
Get on the dance floor and show me what to rap.
2Pac comes back. Rat a Tat Tat Tat.

Mental Health Raps, Writing for Recovery

Stephen Fry Rap

Stephen Fry, he's a manic depressive and I know
why, he's articulate and not shy.
Creative, intelligent, pro homosexual setting a new
precedent of unity understanding, articulate
presenting the Bafta's with panache as if he were
the new president, giving a voice to two educated
minorities, with understanding they will gain
equality for all
a humanitarian empowering the mentally ill,
survived horror at 16 and he's 6ft 5 tall.
An English gent, a comedian, actor and director,
This genius found fame by turning a book into a
play, A Can of Madness would benefit from his
direction I would say,

Someone who understands the insanity and the
creativity, and has turned the tables to empower
himself and his family,

A master of four novels and the Fry and Laurie
series, Blackadder at thirty, when I was a kid.
There was something manic in my mind usurping
my id, Mental health improvements for all and
Chipmunks unite,

A multi media movement to give you some f******
rights. This is the Stephen Fry rap, respect to you
kind Sir,

I wish you no future manic depressive attack,
Lets work together I'm sure we can save lives

Jason Pegler

Curing Madness Rap

Curing this madness has eliminated a lot of
sadness and opened gladness,
Creative energy and freedom from medication,
thanks to an incantation.
I self manifested my own suffering for 12 years,
now I'm super normal... cheers.
Focusing on my music, a new challenge for freeing
myself and creating health.
Well being's now the focus of my life, cutting
through strife like a samurai knife.
My own happiness is determined by the life I
choose and what I peruse,
Making news, leaving clues, empowering fuse, and
giving myself my dues... enthuse...
Looking after Jason Pegler first and clenching my
thirst, forgetting when my mind used to burst.
A higher state of consciousness; being without
using NLP, combining the two is the key.
The power of now is appropriate hear, NLP faces,
instead of hides from fear.
Justice for myself and others have to make their
own,
Whatever movement I lead, it cannot be forced or
better overthrown.
Curing Madness, the phenomenon is among us,
I've proved it works... Don't cuss

Belief becomes reality, creating wisdom by
repetition,
I see a vision coming to fruition,
Curing Madness the everlasting transition.

Mental Health Raps, Writing for Recovery

If you've suffered madness or depression before,
step up and get up on the dance floor

Rappers of the world uniting and curing their
sadness,
Jason Pegler stepping forward having cured my
madness.
The Curing Madness rap is no trap, so clap, stop
being a sap and find a girl to sit on your lap, or if
you're a girl then learn to rap.
The Curing Madness rap is here to map,
Out a positive future for the rest of the world,
Relieving us all from mental illness by believing in
ourselves…
It's up to you to do it and do not discriminate,
Being full of hate and ignorant doesn't work for
pity's sake.
Stay awake and create, if you're in love and ready
to impregnate, find a friend, a confidante,
Get up and choose life forever, don't cop out and
say you can't,
Cause the world is beautiful, I'm sure you'll find,
Give to others your happy well being and then
either incantant, or be spiritual and then repeat this
rap and rewind for the benefit of well being and
man and womankind… Open your mind…

The Curing Madness rap, a tat tat, that's just the
way it is. Things will always stay the same. Some
things are due to change, well being for all, is this
rappers call. A former manic depressive… scared
of a false utopia, not at all!!!

Jason Pegler

Duty

Jason Pegler speaking up for unity it's a duty
Being my self always, cured my self it's a beauty
Patients of the world unite, stand up and fight
Make it right, get your head right, ignite,
empowerment like a billion pounds of dynamite
Cure your self and give a voice to others
Your lovers, brothers listen to manic depressive
album corners
Raskil records are an example of the voice of the
young generation
Rebel Alliance step on the mic becoming the new
sensation
Jason Pegler manically curing mental illness as a
concept
Sion in effect, context is next, just say and **Avarice**
Having free styling don't diss, natural bliss, a can of
madness I don't hiss
I'm telling how it feels to have a manic depression
label
Psychiatry a fraud, I've hit a chord…no drugs
company will silence me
I'll speak out on my own accord, Jason Pegler, mc
Jase, Jay Zee and JCB
We'll all be crazy, it's the nature of humanity and
society
So everyone admit this and more on and help or
make way for your sorority
Jason Pegler will blow you away for eternity to revel
the truth about the excluded
Rather be in prison than a psychiatric patient on
medication, welcome everyone to the new nations.

Mental Health Raps, Writing for Recovery

No stigma and discrimination for those falsely
labelled on these turn tables
I've had enough fables and labels, playing the new
turn tables,
A can of madness open up the pages, I've been
telling this story for ages and ages
An autobiography on manic depression that's
saved my life helping others through this strife

Jason Pegler

GIFTED

We're all gifted, the parameters of modern society
has now shifted,
By using the internet, the consumer is in charge
and we find out what we want,
Free and quickly, the paradigm shift is the new
virtual reality,
We're as gifted as we think, moving away from the
brink.
Society questions your behaviour; you can be your
own saviour,
Focus on your own dreams and they will come true,
Find a peer group that inspires you, we're all gifted
it's true,
Life is full of ups and down, but we make our own
results.
Ignore the insults and consciously trigger your
peaks not troughs.
Eliminate the scoffs and toffs and give to yourself to
forget those knots,
Being gifted is a decision at the end of the day;
positivity comes to those whose dreams they obey.
Wasted talented is a cop out, we all have the will
power,
But are you prepared to put in the work hour after
hour,
Delivering your own gift to yourself and others will
inspire new worlds of wonder,
Embracing fear and failure, bouncing back with
vengeance and thunder.
I'm as gifted as that celebrity I hear you say,
Prove it then and seize your own opportunity today
A one degree shift changes your life over time.

Mental Health Raps, Writing for Recovery

A momentous shift eclipsing the sublime.
G to the i to the f to the t,
e to the d, spells gifted... please let yourself be .....
It ain't up to me... just reminding you of what I
decreed for me.
Jason Pegler back with intentions... a former manic
gifted by my own inventions,
Creativity and self belief, cured myself and turned
over a new leaf.
Stronger than before and more fulfilled, thrilled,
past self manifesting killed,
Gifted and thrilled, gifted and fulfilled, g to the i to
the f to the t, to the e to the d
spells gifted... please let yourself be..... G to the i
to the f to the t ...
Choose to be one of those gifted in society.
It ain't up to me ... just reminded you of what I
decreed for me...

London Streets

Jason Pegler reveals a new science with Renegade
artistry signalling a new dawn for da Rebel Alliance,
London is in a state of chaos with terrorists and
foreign criminals upon us,
What really annoys me is the rich getting richer and
the poor getting poorer,
These fat city cats in their pin-striped suits,
They are the real crooks, and the journalists and
the politicians not the spooks.
Their selfish nature and the way their vanity
jewellery,
Causes our manic depressive attacks, voice
hearing and tomfoolery.
The people won't stand it, the chorus are
expanding.
Self-manifesting the struggle of life, with an urban
life.
Sit back and be stabbed in the back, getting high
on the crack,
Or struggle through adversity, supporting your team
on Saturdays.
A certainty, or absurdity, depends on who you pick,
that's a trick.
For a spick, knife to gun click, impress the chick,
I'm a psycho not sick.
Cut your face with a bic, do weights with a brick, I'll
snap out of it now.
That's a blast from the past; I faced up to my
madness,
And surpassed the oppressed, on the wave of a
new crest.

Mental Health Raps, Writing for Recovery

London's all right now I know, cause I can go with
the flow,
Lead the life of a former manic depressive,
Be an example, not a repressive,
Give a f*** about myself, for once again.
But not put myself upon a different shelf,
By wealth, stealth or even my health,
Just be yourself,
And hold on to that fact being proud of it.
Don't make England a tip, come down from your
next trip,
Let the homeless of London have a kip,
For God's sake cheer up,
This rap it made my girl sick.
Let's rap about flowers and be happy quick

This rap will be over before too long,
So come on everybody join in the fun.
Rap is a force for social good,
Dr Dre, Snoop Dogg and Boyz In The Hood,
Come on all you rappers lets change the world,
Let's join Eminem and bypass The Free World

Jason Pegler

Well I hope you like the second rap album. I wanted to illustrate that writing has been a therapeutic tool for me, even though I spend most of my time focusing on publishing.

The release I feel after writing a rap is profound. I feel creative, energised, positive, happy and as if I have released a lot of built up stress.

I have a lot of other things in my life that relieve stress. E.g. work, playing football, eating healthily, spending time with my family etc... but writing gives me a release in a different way.

It makes me feel like it is ok to be every version of myself and think and write as I do. It makes me feel more real and more like I am part of this world.

So much so that I have been inspired to write a third rap album since starting this book to show how inspirational writing can be for me.

So here it is.

Mental Health Raps, Writing for Recovery

Lyrics from my 3rd album entitled *'The Maddest Rapper In The World'* **Written between February and March 2009.**

Published rap

I am writing this rap and I know it is going to be published,
What a feeling of strength and recognition, not stressed.
Communicating my own madness in my own way,
To make me feel like I fit into society some way.
Manic depressive diagnosis at 17 years of age,
Was revealed to me when I was 18, 6 months later.
Felt like I had been snapped by an alligator and that I was made permanently high like that song ringing in my ears,
'I'm the only one and dominator',
The perpetrator, annihilator, monkey maker, cheese grater, refrigerator,
Boa constrictor, conflicted, humiliated trickster, metaphorically kicked in head. Stop. Turn around.
Open my clickster, then snap back and pull back, lock it and stop. Take a deep breathe with some CBT to stop the anxiety leading to a manic depressive attack,
DMX is back after 15 years, shedding more tears, bipolar too, feel an empathy with you, respect is due,
Will embrace not battle, and hand over my rattle,
Know your name, not going to say it
Like Xzibit when you start selling digits then I'll pay attention to you.

In, out and of the mind, from mania to being at the
beat of a heart.
Get your own house in order before you start
DJ SY and Ratty 'like a bird in The sky flying so
high'
Take me to the fantasia the cartoon please not the
rave,
Then I can get off my knees, reprieve and continue
to help those who are being brave.

Mental Health Raps, Writing for Recovery

Counting Down

Counting Down. Frowning like an upside down clown.
How many raps are there left until my recovery?
Gonna keep writing forever if that's what it takes.
That Robbie on Effexor, what we gonna do?
Gotta help him, but only if he wants to.
Da telepathy don't work through. Fry some eggs for him blim.
Manic not dim.
Sensitive and slim.
Vulnerable not grim.
Anxious, shake your head off Snap back defy gravity, allow depravity, enable empowerment, with a system that works, writing is cathartic, publishing is my therapy.

Feel like a rogue state trooper referring to myself in the tenth person, my business not done, just begun, Google alert, my mind going berserk.
Addicted to work and the internet, worried what people think, my head is on the blink,
Making a bench mark, put my soul on a chopping board,
Hoping the world will evolve and embrace us all, humiliation must stop and the labels must drop,
Stigma goodbye, new world just began.
Everyone is happy, people are content, justice for all, share the food in the world, manage it better, look after the environment, god help us Obama, Jay Z and Puff Daddy, Hollywood unite, Rainman screenwriter join us, then I can reunite with Gus.
The manic guitarist, who burnt out Ash back in the

Jason Pegler

day, when society was ok and I was part of it not an outsider or a Rough Rider, or Dellboy on his hang glider.
Still he got out of the wheelchair and blagged a lift back from the hospital. Avoid the bin, don't sin, or drink gin just the juice, and avoid feeling or causing any abuse.

Counting down from 100, not many to go, hypnosis, tranquillo. Adios bro. Io siento, tomorrow, Yo.

Mental Health Raps, Writing for Recovery

Grooverider

Grooverider... Er... Grooverider.... Still riding on my storm... I can hear your voice, chant and appetiser.
Leave me alone and I'll find her. Insanity is a blinder... Pushed my mind too far...
Now I'm behind her...
My thoughts are on a rewinder... Willed the whole thing cos...
I was sad... Wanted to feel bad... Confidence was low... Opportuntiies were so so...
Made a mistake and I paid for it. Accept that and move on. Gotta be strong. Hate being wrong.
Open up and feel strong.
Until I'm knocked down again, for trying too hard. Gonna get myself up... Add some armour and stuff. Like a polar bear's Pullman, this armours my soul. My own identity and role.
A social entrepreneur with my hand on my heart and the odd paranoia sill tries to pull me apart. Well Ratty saw the second sight. Enough to give anyone a fright.
Playing on my madness no more. Respect who I am that is all.
Never go down that path again. New roads are ahead. Future's so bright I'm having to wear shades, like driving across the Everglades.
For a pic with two crocs, waiting for us. Four months later and I was hit by a bus. Groove Driver. Groove Dyer. Groove Dier. Groove Die. Groovy Groovy Train. Watch out for the Farm. Pigs and Orwell and napalm.
Change your focus then let go. Come with me and

rush with the flow... Absorb the happiness and go. We can all hit the plain. To suggest no-one else can is not fair. The Power of Now ok... We can all achieve being I hear us say... Do not want people to have lost before they start.

Be inclusive like Captain Kirk or we'll all stay berserk. Thanks to Wikipedia we're safe. Google's intense, although it makes a lot of sense.

I'm spent, and relent. Grooverider going out. We can all be happy... Yes... I hear you shout... Join us on the magic roundabout...

Mental Health Raps, Writing for Recovery

Chipmunkapublishing Obama

Writing these raps and its got to be said,
This guy is manic and he is off his head.
Waiting for the testimonies to come in from the
authors,
Providing evidence to show that catharsis and
empowerment are real,
writing some more so I can feel it again, surreal.
It's actually a pleasant exercise as I type away,
Writing in March 09, hope I will finish by May.
Writing is cathartic, I hear you say,
Publishing is empowering I can see this today
Wicpie another acronym like Wacpae oh which one
do we use?
Please peruse, confuse, no, you choose, refuse,
yo,
Focus for a mo, feel the flow, then you'll know,
start writing now and feeling the vibe
enthusiasm's back and happiness is alive,
happiness for others we strive
self indulgence, misery and self manifestation
gone.
Writing and publishing for all will make us one
Internet, Google, for your perusal,
Chipmunkapublishing can help some like the magic
Google.
Time to move on and be the observer,
Observed myself and took a step back
No more stretching on the rack,
for the mental health rat pack
Splickety splat, rat a tat tat
Obama made it 2 pac, so rest in peace,

Jason Pegler

California Love and the mental health publishing niche.

Mental Health Raps, Writing for Recovery

Writing

Writing is cathartic; it has to be said,
Once I was manic, before nuff man dead.
Made myself high from a yearning for more,
Wrote myself in and out of it so got back to before.
Experienced to the fore, what a hell of a life,
Conquered troubles and strife, like shredding butter
through a knife.
Typing on the page is my therapy still,
Thought I'd ended the need when I created Will.
He was in the third person so didn't work,
Hid behind a door, carried on being a jerk.
When I came out, in autobiography, I made my own
style.
A roller coaster ride and peak performed for a while
Anxiety and paranoia returned had to put them to
bed.
Writing out my madness, so it stays in check,
Puts my life into perspective mate, so I'm not a
wreck.
Guaranteed to help me and you I hope,
Better for me than smoking the dope, like an
isotope bloke, hanging a rope in front of the pope
because he couldn't cope, elope. Want that future
that's been paralyzing your life? Nope...
Then write as therapy and let all the baggage out,
write with freedom and it will help no doubt, give
you a fresh start and rejuvenate,
Reassess your life so there's not too much on your
plate, stop you feeling irate, make your own
template, accept your mistakes, perform in a peak
state, don't slate, relate, recover and state. I see he

states, The United States, Tate, Tait, Matthew you
are underrated,

Mental Health Raps, Writing for Recovery

Empowerment

Empowerment is a rap apart. What does this word mean I hear you start? We all know, but none of us can describe it, especially when we need it.
Don't ask me, I am just trying to figure it out and how to rhyme this rap, so it doesn't sound like I'm trapped... rat a tat tat... who wrote that... what's that feeling... rise and shine... matter of fact, empowerment means expanding, growing your mind, feeling stronger, opportunities being longer, not feeling like a wrong-er,
Not feeling the stigma, humiliation gone. Nothing seems wrong, negative cycles disappear like you were drinking a beer, Lets all cheer.
Warmness in your heart, glowing, throwing the perfect dart, 180 degrees and turn your life around, society waits for your breath, sight and sounds.
Empowerment... knowing, meeting kindred spirits, coincidence thrives, meet more positive people,
New days are brighter, rapping gets tighter, lighter, you're a fighter for the empowering process of writing and publishing. Like being born again as if you were the Notorious B.I.G,
standing for peace, what a release, going back to Belize, Nice, forgive my mate Rees, Empowerment speaks, no need to define can feel it, enjoy and unite. Help others fight, empower the others, your mother, your brothers... You're lost... Now you're found... you were living a death... You have helped others too... respect is due for your bravery... Woohoo...Woohoo. Yippede doo...Choo Chooo...

Media

The media process has helped me before. Used to
be nervous, then feared it once more.
Have been misquoted and felt like I was focusing
on the negatives and derivatives.
Media has a style that is all. Best when it's live
makes you feel 10 feet tall.
Then I can get my point of view across and feel like
the boss.
Play the media game all day long must be strong,
they have a job to do, and so do you.
Media, media and mental health
Mental health, mental health and media.
Speaking out for the people with mental illness
Got to be brave so they can have positive thoughts,
Don't get sucked in and show all my warts,
Show I'm a success and then others can feel this is
possible too,
Cathartic empowerment if we're publishing you
Go through the same process me and you.
That's what you do, media volunteering can give
others hope. Local paper, newspaper, radio,
national magazine, TV and radio, international
coverage and internet galore. Google media,
mental health service users all joining together
Help the media reduce the stigma forever and
forever.

Mental Health Raps, Writing for Recovery

Helping that one person helps some more

I had an aim to help another 17 year old manic
depressive. Once I got an email from someone who
said it was him. I cried a grin, took it on the chin, my
head made a din, and my mind was in a spin.
Other people told me *A Can of Madness* helped
them too; glad I survived the ecstasy and didn't
sniff any glue. What was I gonna do?
Try and help more people at the end of the day.
Made my life simple, you know what to say?
Gave me a purpose and something to do,
Justified myself and my new utopian view.
Head came down from the clouds so I grafted at it,
Seven years on we've survived some blips.
Still growing strong and building a brand.
Mental health publishing is therapeutic not grand,
Feel lucky to have created something that does
some good.
Have my ups and downs, but imagine anyone
would.
Always rethinking the best way to do it
Evolving, revolving, involving, resolving
Helping that one person helps some more.
Others feel it too, that's why they come to the fore
Humanity is the key at the end of the day,
Want me to join society and get a job? No way.
Writing and publishing are in my soul and they are
here to stay.
Social entrepreneurship is the Jason Pegler way.
Thank you so much authors for believing in me.
Lets helps some more people and feel that positive
Chi and be back for tea.

Catharsis

Catharsis is so powerful I can feel it in my heart.
It's beating away with my pulse and so strong I can start.
To appreciate the creativity that has healed the wounds,
Insanity humiliation, helping the nation,
Now know my self, with my book on the shelf
Writing again, catharsis once more
An internal mindset sure, but not an addiction or a chore.
Isolated, lonely, full of negative thoughts
Creativity opens and the writing sees the negative and aborts.
A new beginning dawns and the observer is in charge.
Removes the old negative self like a Lomu shoulder barge,
Catharsis recharge... Like an eternal battery.
Catharsis recharge... For Homer its Marge...
Catharsis recharge... Writing and publishing's camouflage, entourage, premier etage, Lance Armstrong inspires as does reportage,
Recovery complete, stand back on my two feet
Feels really neat, unlike the Cuckoo nest's Chief,
Making Murphy's release, catharsis enables peace
And makes life worth living, oneself is forgiven,
A new life is beginning. Catharsis we're winning.

Life Is Worth Living

Life is worth living. Today dawns a new beginning.
People are good and they want to help.
Gotta help ourselves so we can hear others yelp,
Strengthen yourself and inspire like minded folk.
Be the egg to their joke and be a supporting bloke,
Avoid a toke, and getting soaked, and a stroke.
Relax and breathe in, focus on now and you're in.
Reality is living not how you lived or will live.
Enjoy every moment, like Panji playing basketball
for Solent, no need for opponents.
Let life live itself; put your book on your shelf.
Writing, empowerment and publishing combined,
Yes life is worth living I can hear your mind.
Play don't stop, fast forward or rewind,
Then your mood won't get left behind.
When they ask us the question is life worth living?
It is to check how we are it seems harsh not
forgiving,
It's a genuine attempt to see how we are,
From there we are assessed, our minds may be a
mess,
With being strong and forgiving, we can make life
worth living,
Let go of our pain and welcome the rain, let go of
the strain and open the reigns, let the warts out and
stains, stop going insane and join society
somehow, not tomorrow, please do it Now.
Wow… what a feeling… Wow… what a feeling…
I'm living a dreaming… what a glorious feeling…

Standing up now not kneeling,
That has got to be more appealing, and it's healing,
your happiness hits the ceiling... goes through the
ceiling...
Life is not worth leaving... to precious and
magical... to precious and magical... Let the
happiness inside of you... then you can help a
few... Do be do doo... Do be do dooo... Wo..
Wooo.

Mental Health Raps, Writing for Recovery

Recovery

Recovery is a long road for some, a transitional
phase, somewhat of a haze and a maze,
Although there is logic to writing on the page
Whatever your rage or age or cage, you can
somehow gauge.
Recovery is happening now, raise your eye brows,
Allow, disembowel, wash your face and dry with a
towel,
A refreshing start, like one's own Exchange and
Mart, pulling together not apart, anymore, recovery,
Recovery, once more, coming to the fore, life no
longer a chore, or a bore, or couped up in a drawer,
soul's strength has a new core...

Social Entrepreneur

This poetry is a kind of iambic pentameter,
A rap crossing genres for empowerment for all ya.
Memoirs, autobiographies, fiction and poetry
Carers, Survivors, Patients, Service Users United.
Delighted, ignited, blighted, Catullus was stranded
From the Millenium Dome to Rome and your
garden gnome.
Rapping this poetry for the human race to save
face,
Learned how to tie up my shoelace in four hours so
I could get to the next place
O to the C to the D, rap is a cathartic tool for me,
my poetry.
Rapping for 8 billion years and taking a first breath
Now start again as I have still got some energy left,
Rapping now for the mental health generation
again.
Someone's got to do it next, please I am tired
Eminem,
Iambic again, Pentameter again and again,
Dr Dre please provide some beats and help MC
Jase speak,
Just another way to speak to get the word off the
streets.
Time to advance, not retreat, rhyming so tight I am
running off my feet
Neat beats a feat, with social entrepreneurship
lyrics.

Mental Health Raps, Writing for Recovery

Love

Rapping for love and the human race
Time to say goodbye JCB, this is MC Jase.
Two of my alter ego's give way to the third, Jason
Pegler, making way for a touchdown from the
refrigerator.
A rap for love and humanity is the place to go,
All you need is love and then go with the flow.
Chipmunka love going out to you now,
A little nervous and afraid then I will show you how
A chance to give yourself a voice and let others be
heard.
Catharsis and empowerment take over from the
manic and absurd,
Love your voice to be heard, Love the healing
process of the written word.
Feel your heart beating strong, something going on,
Feel your heart beating strong, nothing going
wrong.
Love, peace and unity and Chipmunka's unite,
Bringing people together from all walks in life,
We've all got something in common,
Struggled through adversity and through writing
want to recover
There's a long road ahead, but some of us have
made it,
Time to hold on and help others embrace it
Feel the love now and others will relate a bit
Time to feel strong, love… Yes love is going on…

Jason Pegler

Thanks you so much for reading my raps. That was a cathartic and empowering process for me. I wanted to experience the writing process and try to define my feelings and thought processes whilst writing this book to show how it helped me.

I wrote the lyrics to the third rap album in just a few days in March 09. I just wanted to show people and myself that when creativity is at a high, then a lot can be achieved and a lot of positive writing can take effect. The lyrics to my third rap album are in my opinion more positive than the lyrics from the second album. This in my view is because I was set on finishing them in a short period of time and visualised the completion of the album.

This visualisation gave me more determination to finish the task and as I knew I was writing as part of this book which has a positive theme; the theme and content of the raps joined in with the cathartic and empowering process.

Of course, everyone has their own writing style and it does not matter what mood we are in when we write as some of the best and most positive writing can come out of the most painful times.

Mental Health Raps, Writing for Recovery

Lyrics from one song from my 4th Rap Album entitled:

'Empowerment - Mental Health Raps'

Mental Health Raps are coming so fast out of my mind, got to get them out for my sanity

43 now in this book alone, as each one comes out my sanity has grown

Stepping back into reality, Eminem I know I am no parity, but your inspiration gives me clarity,

Thank you for helping me finding my sanity and temporarily removing my insanity

With my madness lower my positive personality can thrive, my ego takes a nose dive, my creativity produces as much honey as a bee hive, I can envision a better world where I can strive.

Mental health raps open the door for others to thrive, Google and chipmunka unite, rappers of the world delight, survivor writers ignite and the mentally ill are able to help each others in their plight,

We will never give up this fight, it continues when we are all asleep, night after night, equality for mental health patients around the world and justice for all. Utopia is reached and like millions of slim shadies happily bleached in that video, respect is

due, mental health raps.... Opening the creativity
taps, giving you Chipmunkapublishing books on
your laps, and your kindle downloads,
empowerment, explodes.

Mental Health Raps, Writing for Recovery

Nearly Half Way There

44 gone that's 46 to go
Once this one is done then we're half way to 90.
My mind will nearly be nearly half way fixed
100 raps will be done
Then a million more just in my head or my typing
fingers will be dead
What's this rap about? I hear myself shout.
I am bipolar and its here to say. Never gonna go
away.
My soul is on the web and google has me exposed
The more I get in the public eye the more my manic
energy flows, I broke my own nose, I took the drugs
myself, psychiatry took me in as I made my life a
mess, everything's my fault although somehow I
feel blessed.

Diversity's just made me feel less stressed. A
Dance Troup to empower the young people.
Positive role models for all to see, this bipolar is not
going to take me, manic depression got a hold of
my spirit, still fighting through it, humanity gives me
hope, there are others I can help, the stronger I can
stay myself the more potential I have for social
good. Improve neighbourhoods, we all have duties
as citizens, can only support so many as its so
intense. Write, publish, PR, improve the life of
others, open the door to my manic brothers,
personality opens doors and character keeps it
open. Sugar Hill Gang know the score as does that
last quote from Sir Alan.

Jason Pegler

You Down with JCB?

You down with JCB yeah you know me
J is for the Jason. C is for the crazy and B is for the
bipolar. J is my real name and C is my life before
my bipolar. My bipolar is the rest of me that invades
the present like a Hedda Gabbler essay. Want to
learn about it but don't see the point of it. It exists
and then ii doesn't. Invented like my alter ego. It's a
frame of mind.

Get real and not reality. Be yourself, know thyself,
be creative and jump out of the abyss, do not
drown in it, take it head on and split. Tackle get up
and tackle again. Like Martin Johnson training is
my kind of way of explaining the mental strength
needed, embrace, not heeded.

Mental Health Raps, Writing for Recovery

Lyrics from one song from my 5th Rap Album entitled Mad Ghetto

Mad Ghetto

Blowing up world trade Biggie scrumming like Nieto
Gloucester boy through and through me mad
ghetto in tow.
More than Springbok intensity with Gloucester pride
Jay Z and 2 Pac and Coolio's slippery ride
Ice Cube, Dre and Snoop lyrical wizards and Dre's
beats to match
Eazy E's no Studio Gangsta respect to him R.I.P.
Eminem elaborating on urban myth and legends
Sugar Hill Gang and Manic G now to the manic JP
Boogie Down Productions and KRS one
2 Live Crew seems like yesterday like my life has
just begun
Avoiding conflict now and embracing people and
the world
Even playing football my sportsmanship comes to
the fore
20,000 hardcore really did knock at my door

The Mad Ghetto Rap is one of a kind, empowering
mental health survivors and carers to make the
most of their matching chimes. Mad ghetto on the
sublime, reality used to be a friend of time. My
rap... Mine... You rap too... That's fine... With the
beat in time...